'brave, true and touching'
— Margaret Drabble

'ingenuous in spirit and
well-crafted in form'
— *The Stage*

'Strikingly original and carefully
woven . . . refreshing and genuine . . .
expertly turning a reclusive spinster
from a bygone day into the strong-
minded philosopher, rugged
individualist and delicious ironist that
she clearly was...A production of rare
integrity'
— *The Scotsman* (Critics Choice)

'A warm and delicious
paean to the bibliophile in
us all'
— *The List*

Emily Dickinson & I
The Journey of a Portrayal

Emily Dickinson & I

The Journey of a Portrayal

for Paul Sagar Campbell
(1912–1995)

Emily Dickinson & I

The Journey of a Portrayal

a one woman play about
writing, acting and getting
into Emily Dickinson's dress

conceived by Jack Lynch
written by Edie Campbell & Jack Lynch

BLACK
SPRING
PRESS

Published in 2005 by Black Spring Press Ltd
Curtain House
134–146 Curtain Road
London EC2A 3AR

www.blackspringpress.co.uk

ISBN 0-948238-31-3

A full CIP record for this book is available from the British Library

Design Hanna Sundén
Cover photography Andreas Larsson
Typeset in Minion by Dexter Haven Associates Ltd, London
Printed and bound in Spain by Graficas Viking, Barcelona

CONTENTS

Foreword

Margaret Drabble

I first saw Edie Campbell's portrayal of Emily Dickinson in an intimate theatre in Guildford, and vividly remember the excitement of that evening. The performance was brave, true and touching, and the unfolding story was easy to follow and gripping to watch. It is a story of obsession, identification, admiration and respect. The background information about Dickinson's life and work is conveyed so subtly and effortlessly that one realises only later how much has been packed into this short and personal evocation of one of America's greatest but most enigmatic poets. The playwright has managed to dramatise, without betrayal or exaggeration, the life of a recluse, whose outward life was remarkable for its lack of events, but whose inner life was of a fierce, at times melo-dramatic, intensity. Using only the simplest of props, she manages to evoke the physical presence of the poet, and to suggest the small Amherst community in which she lived. Like Dickinson herself, she has pared down her message to its essentials. Technically, this is a remarkable achievement.

Edie Campbell discloses, within the play itself, both the nature of her obsession, and her long struggle to find an appropriate approach to her subject matter—an approach which took nearly twenty years to discover, and which involved many false starts and periods of despondency. Campbell's own presence on stage and in the text is not intrusive or indulgent, for it appears as a necessary embodiment of her search. Recent biographers, such as Richard Holmes in his pioneering work *Footsteps*,[1] have created a precedent for using the difficulties, even the failures of research, as part of the plot of their work: this play carries the process one step further, by including the person of the seeker as a physical image of the one who is sought. The quest for Dickinson is interwoven with Campbell's questioning of the artistic role, and the contradictions of the artistic temperament—a temperament that paradoxically combines an urge to display and an urge to withdraw and conceal.

The decision to restrict the use of the poet's voice to the words of her own poems and letters must be correct. Inventing dialogue or commentary for such an eccentric and powerful writer would have been an impossible task, for her use of language is unique, and any imitation could only emerge as

---

[1] Viking Penguin, London, 1985.

parody. The poems incorporated in the play are carefully chosen from the wealth of Dickinson's oeuvre, and will encourage the reader or spectator to seek for more. The poems are brilliant, elliptical, condensed: each one requiring further reflection. They shine out like jewels from the text, which provides a fine setting for them. Edie Campbell has managed to pay a very personal tribute to the writer whose work has haunted her for so long, while at the same time allowing her to speak for herself, in her own words. It is a very ingenious solution to an unusual dramatic and biographical problem. The solution was found with the support and help of friends and colleagues, whose suggestions are incorporated into the fabric and narrative of the play, but at the end, the final impression is of the poet herself, speaking out loud and clear, across time, to each new audience. And this is what the playwright would wish.

MARGARET DRABBLE

JANUARY 2005

Preface

Jack Lynch

'There she is.'

Thus opens the play *Emily Dickinson &I, the journey of a portrayal*.

When Edie first approached me with her idea of a one-woman play regarding Emily Dickinson, 'using only her words', it seemed like a good idea. I came to understand, rather quickly, the difficulty of such an approach. Someone else might have the genius to do it successfully, but it certainly lies beyond my (our) reach. What quickly came into focus, though, was Edie's passion for Emily.

And there it was. It was Edie's 'love affair with this woman' that inspired me. It was Edie's struggle to write a play about her idol that was worth pursuing. I suddenly realised I was not interested in Edie 'becoming' Emily Dickinson, nor did I want to put Emily Dickinson on the stage.

Edie, however, was having none of this. When she realised I was suggesting that her story be told along side Emily's, the answer was a flat out, 'No!'

We never come to an artist's work without our own historical, social and psychological baggage in hand. The more I thought about Edie and her relationship with Emily as a subject for a play, the more I became curious about what it is that draws a person to a particular author's works, that relationship between writer and reader, between the artist and the viewer. And if one is drawn (or repelled) by an artist's work, what does that say about the viewer? Edie and I thus became engaged in a process of mixing the biographical with the autobiographical, the relationship between the poet and the reader who are of different times, different countries, different disciplines.

While I was a student at the Naropa Institute (now University) in Boulder, Colorado, one of our tasks as performance artists was to create a 'personal journey piece'. We were steeped in the practice of sitting (both as a meditation practice and as an artistic metaphor) with what was arising in the moment and trusting the constant arrival of 'now' to be the palette from which to paint. Those teachers at Naropa encouraged us to continually listen to the thing that was being created, without agenda, because 'it', as its own entity, would inform the artist what the next step might be, but only if the artist was truly listening and able to respond. So, in our artistic practice, we were also learning how to be 'response-able' human beings. We would begin making work by asking, 'What has brought me to this moment in time?' I have carried that with me ever since.

It is through this process that the script of *Emily Dickinson & I* came to be, by trusting what was unfolding through improvisation as we travelled into the present unknown; by asking what brought Edie to this moment in time with her subject. What emerged was a play about the play that never happened, a meditation on writing, acting, and getting into Emily Dickinson's dress.

JACK LYNCH
BINSCOMBE
JANUARY 2005

Acknowledgements

The process of writing, performing and producing
Emily Dickinson & I owes a great deal to the
inspiration, constructive criticism, advice and
practical help of many people both in the US and
the UK. Among these, we would particularly like to
recognise the following: Becky Swift, whose shared
passion for Emily has been a driving force throughout the process. Jean Newkirk and Annejet Campbell
each fashioned an excellent replica of Emily's dress.
Seb Williams created the original lighting design
and was a real life-saver. Malcolm Crowthers took
the striking photos that we used in our publicity.
Robert Hastings, from his first viewing of the play,
suggested we publish it and then made it all happen.
Designer Hanna Sundén truly captured the spirit of
the script for the book cover. Fellow actors, playwrights and directors at the University of Iowa,
particularly Pauline Tyer, listened to and encouraged
us to keep at it ('Don't give up, it's a good idea').
And Margaret Drabble, whose words have been a
continual blessing.

We would also like to thank Amherst College
Library (Archives and Special Collections), Harvard
University Press, Susan Chambers, Ron Clark,
Rebecca Clouse, Mark Dean, Scott DeShong, Cindy
Dickinson, Kathleen Diffley, Anne Flammang, Peter
Florence, Lee Grumett, John Harris, Michael
Holroyd, Jody Hovland, David Lavender, John
Locke, Roger Martin, Katie Matthews, Neil
McPherson, John Montague, Kate Napier, Sarah
Smyth, Bill and Margo Stallybrass, Clive Swift,
Elisabeth Tooms, Piers Torday, Sally Vaughan, Craig
Wolffis, and last, but not least, Frits Philips and our
families. And with apologies to William Luce and
Jamie Fuller.

EDIE CAMPBELL & JACK LYNCH
BINSCOMBE
JANUARY, 2005

photo Mark Dean

EDIE CAMPBELL obtained her BA from the Oxford Poly, trained at the Guildford School of Acting and then spent nine years in the US where, among other things, she did quite a bit of acting and received her MA in English Literature from the University of Iowa. She now lives in the UK with Jack, performing *Emily Dickinson & I* and their second play, *Cloning Mary Shelley*. She is also a proof-reader and works with medical students using medical role-play.

photo Jill Tobin

JACK LYNCH, born in Iowa City, Iowa, is the Co-founder and Artistic Director of LynchPin Productions. He trained in theatre, with an emphasis in movement and performance, at the University of Iowa (MFA), and the Naropa University, in Boulder, Colorado (BA). Jack is currently involved in various writing projects, medical role-play, and teaching at the Guildford School of Acting Conservatoire.

Emily Dickinson & I was first performed as *My Life Has Stood*—a slightly modified quotation from Poem 754—at the Mill Studio, Guildford, Surrey, on 8 December 1999. It was directed by Jack Lynch. The lighting design was by Seb Williams. Replica of Emily's dress by Jean Newkirk and Annejet Campbell. Performed by Edie Campbell.

Running Time: 90 minutes

Time: December, 1999

Cast: Edie, an actor

The play has been performed extensively, including at the Edinburgh Fringe, Brighton Fringe, Hay Festival of Literature, Royal Society of Literature, the Cheltenham Festival of Literature and the Finborough Theatre, London.

THE STAGE IS BARE EXCEPT FOR A FOLDING
SCREEN *USR*; EDIE ENTERS CARRYING LARGE
BUNDLE OF PAPERS; SHE TURNS *CS*; FACES
AUDIENCE; DROPS PAPERS ONTO FLOOR;
SLIGHT PAUSE

There she is.

PAUSE

Emily Elizabeth Dickinson.
Poet.

KNEEL TO PAPERS AS IF READING A
GRAVESTONE

Born 1830.
Died 1886,
of kidney failure called 'Brights'
disease.

TEACHER VOICE ON 'BRIGHTS', MAKING THE
SOUND 'BRIGHT', ROLLING THE 'R'

Born and died in the same house,
the Homestead,
in Amherst, Massachusetts.
Built by Emily's grandfather,

the Homestead had the distinction of
being the first brick house in Amherst.

After her grandfather's death,
Emily's parents settled in the
Homestead and had three children:
Austin,
Emily,
and Lavinnia.
Vinnie.

STAND

I don't have an older brother,
but I do have a younger sister:
Digna.
Diggie.

Like Emily,
I was born in my grandfather's house,
which is in Eindhoven, Holland,
my mother being Dutch.
My Dad was Canadian.
He died five years ago of something
very similar to Alzheimer's called
Binswangers disease.

'Binswangers…?'
Now there's a word for you.

Emily loved words.
They were her passion.

> *I don't know of anything so mighty. There are
> those to which I lift my hat when I see them.*

'Binswangers'.

BEGIN TO EXIT…

Emily would have loved it.

**ENTER WITH STACK OF EMILY DICKINSON
BOOKS; CROSS TO *DSL***

I am in love with Emily Dickinson.
Infatuated.

PLONK BOOKS ON FLOOR

Obsessed.

**EXIT; ENTER CARRYING SMALL WOODEN
CHEST; CROSS TO *DSR***

Emily is considered America's foremost
female poet.
She wrote one thousand seven hundred
and seventy-five poems
only seven of which were published,
anonymously,
during her lifetime.
The rest were discovered by her sister,
Vinnie,
many sewn into little booklets,
in a little chest

PLACE CHEST ON FLOOR

at the foot of Emily's bed after her
death,

EXITING...

of 'Brights' disease.

**BEGIN SPEAKING OFF-STAGE; ENTER WITH
MANNEQUIN; CROSS TO *USRC* AND PLACE
MANNEQUIN IN FRONT OF SCREEN**

I am an actress.
I'm not a playwright.

**SET DOWN MANNEQUIN, TURNING IT TO FACE
AUDIENCE ON FOLLOWING**

> And I'm not a dressmaker, either.
> (So what am I trying to do?)

STAND *SL* OF MANNEQUIN

> My mother's the dressmaker.
> This is her at 18.

**PUT RIGHT ARM AROUND SHOULDERS OF
MANNEQUIN LIKE AN OLD FRIEND; LOOK AT
MANNEQUIN, NOTICE MANNEQUIN'S BREASTS;
LOOK AT OWN BREASTS**

> Spot the, uh, family resemblance?

> When I told a friend I was trying to
> write a play about Emily, he asked
> what the set would consist of.

CROSS TO CHEST

> I said:
> 'Oh, I don't know…
> probably a desk…

a chair...
and a little chest...
(that would be me).

OPEN CHEST AND DISCOVER BUST OF EMILY

Oh, and look...

PRESENT BUST FOR AUDIENCE

A little bust.
Emily.

PLACE BUST ON FLOOR *SL* OF CHEST

And this

REMOVING DRESS FROM CHEST, PRESENTING DRESS FOR AUDIENCE

is Emily's dress.

Well,
not really.

SEE PAPERS *DSC*; THROW DRESS ONTO LEFT SHOULDER; CROSS TO PAPERS

I have been trying to write a play
about Emily Dickinson for the last
fourteen years.
And that

INDICATING PILE OF PAPERS

is as far as I've got
in all of its various and sundry forms.

I know what I don't want to do.

GO TO STACK OF BOOKS

I don't want to write a piece of
historical fiction,
like this…

**HOLD UP *THE DIARY OF EMILY DICKINSON* BY
JAMIE FULLER**

or a play like this,

**HOLD UP *THE BELLE OF AMHERST* BY WILLIAM
LUCE**

in which the playwright puts words in
the poet's mouth.

That's what I don't want to do.

What I want
is to be Emily's mouthpiece.

But how do I perform that
without getting in her way?

**DROP THE TWO BOOKS IN FRONT OF THE PILE
IN MILD FRUSTRATION**

I'll come back to that.

CROSS TO MANNEQUIN

(I'm always coming back to that.)

PUT DRESS ON MANNEQUIN

I first *met* Emily in 1980
when I picked a slim volume of her
poetry
off the school library shelves.
I'd never heard of her before.
She certainly wasn't on the
curriculum.
I read that slim volume from cover to
cover in one sitting and

I
was
hooked.
The first poem I read was number
seven-four-seven.
Emily didn't title her poems, by the
way. Her editors have numbered and
dated them, according to the dramatic
changes in her handwriting during her
life.

RETRIEVE *EMILY DICKINSON: THE COMPLETE*
POEMS, **FROM CHEST; FIND POEM**

Poem seven-four-seven

READ

It dropped so low in — my Regard —
I heard it hit the Ground —
And go to pieces on the Stones
At bottom of my Mind —

Yet blamed the Fate that flung it — less
Than I denounced Myself,
For entertaining Plated Wares
Upon my Silver Shelf —

CROSS *USC* AND FACE MANNEQUIN

> Thus began my
> love affair
> with this woman.

REGARD BOOK OF POEMS; CROSS *DSC*

> Three years later
> my Dad gave me this volume,
> *Emily Dickinson: The Complete Poems*,
> for Christmas, 1983.
> He gave great books for Christmas.
> I loved that about him.
>
> At the time I was in a production of
> *Look Back in Anger*
> and I was head over heels in love with
> my leading man.
> Unfortunately,
> he was in love with someone else.
> I was heartbroken.
> I found myself turning to Emily for
> comfort
> and discovered that her words
> expressed all my feelings
> better
> than I could.
> And ever since

HOLD BOOK AGAINST HEART

> I have taken Emily's poems
> and measured all my life's experiences
> against them.

FROM MEMORY...

> *I Measure every Grief I meet*
> *With narrow, probing, Eyes —*
> *I wonder if It weighs like Mine —*
> *Or has an Easier size.*

LOOK AT BOOK; PLACE BOOK ON FLOOR *SR* OF PILE OF PAPERS

> 1985.
> Oxford Poly.

EXIT

> I am in another play,

ENTER WITH SMALL STOOL

> *Pride and Prejudice*,
> and in love again.

PLACE STOOL *SL* **OF MANNEQUIN**

Unsuccessfully.

EXIT

And I discover that one of the
directors,

ENTER WITH SEWING BOX

Becky,
is as passionate about Emily as I am.

**SIT ON STOOL, OPEN SEWING BOX AND TAKE
OUT PINS**

We decide to write a play about her.
Well,
Becky will write it,
I will perform it,
and we'll both do the research.

I tell Becky there already is a one-
woman play about Emily,
The Belle of Amherst,
by William Luce.

LOOK AT STACK OF BOOKS

I read it to her.

It's not that it's…
…horrible
It's just not the real Emily.
The undiluted Emily.
Our Emily…
Which is, of course, the *real* Emily.

PAUSE; LOOK AT STACK OF BOOKS

However…
my Dad had been very moved by the
play when he and I had seen it the year
before.

START PINNING DRESS

In the play,
when Emily's favourite nephew,
Gilbert,
dies at the age of seven,
Dad wept.
It took him back to the time his little
sister,
Edith

(my namesake),
died when she was five and Dad was
seven,
in the influenza pandemic of 1919
as it swept across the Canadian
prairies.
When little Edith died,
the ground was too frozen to bury her.
So my grandparents kept her in her
coffin
on the porch
and oiled her little body
every day
until the spring thaw.

STOP PINNING DRESS

Emily once wrote to a grieving friend:

> *I do not ask if you are 'better' — because split
> lives — never 'get well' — but the love of friends
> — sometimes helps the Staggering — when the
> Heart has on it's great freight.
> The first section of Darkness is the densest,
> Dear — After that,
> Light trembles in —*

RESUME PINNING

1986.
Becky and I are both living and
working in London and a feverish
period of Emily research ensues.
We reread all one thousand seven
hundred and seventy-five poems,
often calling each other up at all hours
of the day and night—
'Have you read number ten seventy-
two?
What's that about?
And what about six forty?
Oh, and two ninety-three,
we must put that one in.'

Becky and I read all the biographies we
can get our hands on.
And in them we discover...
Emily's letters.
There are one thousand and forty-nine
of her letters still in existence. The rest
have been lost or deliberately
destroyed.
Those one thousand and forty-nine are
considered to be
a mere *tenth*
of her correspondence
and she wrote to at least 93 people.

Just think what she could have done with e-mail.

**REACH FOR CUP OF TEA UNDER STOOL...
NOT THERE; LOOK FOR IT UNDER AND
AROUND STOOL; NOT THERE; SEE IT OFF-
STAGE LEFT...**

Speaking of which, did you know that if you do a search for Emily Dickinson on the web you get over 339,000 hits?

But I digress.

EXIT

Becky and I wanted our play to debunk the popular myths about Emily.
To separate the myths from the facts.

**TRANSFORM INTO COLLEGE TEACHER, WITH
HALF-MOON READING SPECTACLES ON A
CHAIN, SPEAKING WITH HIGH-PITCHED
CLIPPED SPEECH**

So,
what *do* we know about Emily Dickinson?

ENTER WITH OVERHEAD PROJECTOR

> To review…
> and I hope you're taking notes because
> there will be an exam:

**SWITCH ON OHP AND BEGIN LECTURE,
PROJECTING BULLET-POINT NOTES**

> We know that she was born in 1830
> and died in 1886 at the Homestead in
> Amherst, Massachusetts;
> That she left Amherst only five times
> during her life;
> That the longest period of time she
> spent away from home was when she
> twice went to Boston for six months to
> be under a doctor's care for eye trouble
> so severe she feared losing her sight;
> That among her favourite books were
> Shakespeare, the King James Bible

DELIGHTED SIGH

> and Milton;
>
> That she hated housework but loved to
> bake; her father would eat *no* bread but
> hers;

That she played the piano and
improvised her own tunes, one of
which she called 'The Devil';
That she had an intense...

LOOKING FOR THE RIGHT WORD...

friendship...
with a young woman called Sue, which
became increasingly complicated after
Sue married Emily's brother, Austin,
and moved into the Evergreens next
door to the Homestead;
That she had her poems rejected for
publication by Thomas Wentworth
Higginson;
That hardly any of her contemporaries
could see the genius in her poetry and
none of her family and few of her
friends knew of her vocation as a poet;
That in her early thirties she stopped
going to church;
That she suffered a severe emotional
crisis;
And that she became a recluse,
receiving the company of only a few
chosen people;
That after her father's death she wore

white almost exclusively;
That her brother, Austin, had a 13-year
affair with a young woman called
Mabel…
26 years his junior.

SNIFF

Interestingly, Mabel was the first to
publish Emily's poems after Emily's
death even though Mabel and Emily
never met face to face;
That the night of her nephew Gilbert's
death was the first time Emily set foot
in her brother's house in 18 years, even
though Austin lived next door;
That she fell in love late in her life
with Judge Otis Philip Lord and had
that love returned;
That she died at the age of 55 of
Brights disease.

Even during Emily's lifetime, myth
rushed in to provide explanations for
the peculiarities in Emily's behaviour.
On first arriving in Amherst, 23-year-
old Mabel (Austin's mistress) wrote to
her parents:

**CROSS DOWN *CS*, TRANSFORM INTO MABEL
WITH AMERICAN ACCENT DURING FIRST LINE**

'I must tell you about the character of
Amherst. It is a lady whom the people
call the Myth. She seems to be the
climax of all the family oddity. She has
not been seen outside of her own house
in 15 years, except once to see a new
church, when she crept out at night, &
viewed it by moonlight. No one who
calls upon her mother & sister ever see
her, but she allows little children, once
in a great while, to come in, when she
gives them cake or candy, for she is
very fond of little ones. But more often
she lets down the sweetmeat by a
string, out of a window, to them. She
dresses wholly in white, & her mind is
said to be perfectly wonderful. She
writes finely, but no one ever sees her.
Isn't that like a book? No one knows
the cause of her isolation, but of course
there are dozens of reasons assigned.'

RETURN TO OHP AS TEACHER

Isn't it interesting that this very Mabel
(Austin's mistress) was to publish three
volumes of Emily's poetry and one of
her letters and travel across the United
States on the lecture circuit, giving
talks about Emily?

Now, I have with me a copy of the only
known photograph of Emily Dickinson,
taken when she was 17 or 18.

PLACE ON OHP

But, there is another one,
taken,
if it is of her,

PLACE ON OHP

when she was 30.
It was found by a book-seller in New
York City some 40 years ago. Someone,
not Emily, has written
'Emily Dickinson 1860'
across the back.
Now,
there were several Emily Dickinsons in
the vicinity of Amherst at the time.
What do you think?

PLACE TRANSPARENCY OF BOTH PHOTOS
ON OHP[1]

Bearing in mind that these two
photographs were taken at least 12
years apart,
compare the eyes,
and the spacing between them.
And the nose.
But most especially the mouth,
the shape
of
the lips.

Well,
I don't know about you,
but I'm convinced.

Unfortunately,
that second photograph was
discredited some ten years ago.
But I don't care.
I'm still convinced.
And a new one has recently been
discovered.
But I don't think it looks like her at all
so I'm not even going to show it to you.

---

[1] For copyright reasons these cannot be reproduced here.

EXIT WITH OHP

> Now, I trust you'll spend the evening
> revising, because the exam starts
> tomorrow morning at 11 o'clock
> *sharp*.

**BEGIN SPEAKING OFF-STAGE; ENTER AS EDIE
WITH MUG OF TEA AND SIT ON STOOL**

> Those are the facts.
>
> What are the myths?
> The gossip?
> The things most people have heard
> about Emily,
> if they've heard anything at all?
> That her father was an oppressive
> tyrant...

**TRANSFORM INTO 1st GOSSIP — MISS
BREATHLESS**

> '...and her mother a vacuous fool, and
> that's why she became a recluse.'

TRANSFORM INTO 2nd GOSSIP — MRS SNOOT

'Oh, no, dear: she fell in love with the Reverend Charles Wadsworth, who happened to be happily married, and had her heart broken, and that's why she became a recluse.'

TRANSFORM INTO 3RD GOSSIP — MR KNOWITALL

'No, no, no. She was in love with Samuel Bowles, the literary man, who happened to be married, and she had her heart broken and that's why she became a recluse.'

BREATHLESS

'Of course, there is the rumour that she was in love with her sister-in-law Sue, and had her heart broken and that's why she became a recluse.'

KNOWITALL

'No, no, no, it wasn't Sue. It was a friend of Sue's, Kate Scott Anthon, and she had her heart broken and that's why she became a recluse.'

SNOOT

'Well, you know she wore white
because she knew she'd never be a
bride.'

BREATHLESS

'Well, at least we can all agree she was
simply...Nuts!'

TRANSFORM BACK TO EDIE

Did it never occur to such people that
perhaps Emily knew she was a genius?
That her ability to write,
her gift of poetry,
meant so much to her that she would
do anything not to lose it?
That she took her vocation as a poet
seriously and dedicated her life to her art?
That she withdrew from the world
because of the richness of her inner
life?
Among her contemporaries Emily
could find no one to match her
intellectually.
She wrote:

All men say 'What' to me.

MOVE TO PILE OF PAPERS *CS*

Perhaps she took Ralph Waldo
Emerson's words to heart when he
wrote that the poet
'must embrace solitude as a bride'.
Perhaps she took his words literally
and that's why she wore white.

**SQUAT AND SEARCH THROUGH PAPERS FOR
EACH OF THE FOLLOWING QUOTES**

She wrote that she

READ

shunned Men and Women [because] *they talk
of Hallowed things, aloud—and embarrass my
Dog—*

When her brother, Austin, was living
and working in Boston,
homesick and lonely,
she wrote to him with envy:

READ

> *if you talk with no one, you are amassing*
> *thoughts which will be bright and golden for*
> *those you left at home* — we *meet our friends,*
> *and a constant interchange* wastes tho't *and*
> *feeling, and we are then obliged to* repair *and*
> renew —

Or listen to this:
words from writers who are our
contemporaries, all quoted in the
London *Times*:

Julie Parsons:

READ

'I like being cut off. I like being on my
own so much so that I'm worried I
might abandon people altogether.'

Or Jake Arnott:

READ

'You have to be detached, and it can
make you sad and lonely, but I love
being reclusive. I think you have to
keep a certain amount of emptiness in
you in order to fill it with prose.'

Or this, from the Canadian poet Anne Michaels:

READ

'The act of writing is so solitary, so silent, so reclusive, to talk too much about it is anathema.'

Emily's sister, Vinnie, always insisted that Emily suffered no love-disappointment,
that her gradual reclusiveness was 'only a happen'.

FIND POEM IN BOOK AND READ

There is a solitude of space
A solitude of sea
A solitude of death, but these
Society shall be
Compared with that profounder site
That polar privacy
A soul admitted to itself —
Finite infinity.

So,

SLAM BOOK CLOSED AND SET ON FLOOR *DSL* **OF PILE OF PAPERS**

> Becky and I had a brilliant idea for our play,
> Instead of dressing Emily in white,
> we were going to dress her in Red!
> Not a woman constantly on the edge of
> a nervous breakdown,
> but a Strong,
> Courageous,
> Passionate Woman
> who knew her own mind and made her
> own decisions with her eyes wide open:

STAND AND MOVE *SL*

> *My Life had stood—a Loaded Gun—*

INDICATE DRESS WITH RIGHT HAND LIKE A BIG STAGE INTRODUCTION

> Emily in a Red Dress.

STAGE/DRESS GOES RED

> *All men say 'What' to me.*

CROSS TO *SR* SIDE OF MANNEQUIN

That was our Emily.
That was what Becky and I wanted to
put on the stage.
We knew what we wanted to say,
but not how to say it.
We realised that in order for people to
be able to follow what we were trying
to do, we would need extensive
programme notes
and our thesis on sale in the foyer.

We got stuck.

CROSS TO STOOL, SIT

Looking back,
I guess we were putting words in
Emily's mouth, creating yet another
myth:
Emily in a Red Dress.

Hardly the real Emily.

Listen to this.

**THROUGHOUT THE FOLLOWING POEM, LIGHTS
IMPERCEPTIBLY CROSS-FADE BACK FROM RED
TO NORMAL SETTINGS**

FROM MEMORY

> *Dare you see a Soul* at the White Heat?
> *Then crouch within the door —*
> *Red — is the Fire's common tint —*
> *But when the vivid Ore*
> *Has vanquished Flame's conditions,*
> *It quivers from the Forge*
> *Without a color, but the light*
> *Of unanointed Blaze.*
>
> *Least Village has its Blacksmith*
> *Whose Anvil's even ring*
> *Stands symbol for the finer Forge*
> *That soundless tugs — within —*
> *Refining these impatient Ores*
> *With Hammer, and with Blaze*
> *Until the Designated Light*
> *Repudiate the Forge —*

But how to portray that
without getting in her way?

PAUSE; LOOK AT MANNEQUIN, THEN BACK OUT

I'll come back to that.

RETURN TO PINNING DRESS

1987.
I get engaged to an American and go
to the Guildford School of Acting.
Emily gets put on the shelf.

1988.
My sister Diggie marries and moves to
Sweden.
I marry and move to America.

1989.
I am somewhere in the American
Midwest.

Iowa City, Iowa, to be precise.
I always thought that was such a funny
place name,

PLAYING WITH THE VOWELS IN I-O-WA

I-o-wa City, I-o-wa.
I never knew it existed until a friend
wrote me a letter from there,
about Emily oddly enough.
And then I end up living there for nine
years.

In I-o-wa City, I-o-wa,
I — Am
thousands of miles away from my
home in London…
my friends…
my family…

Emily's family hardly ever left home,
and when they did,
they couldn't wait to return.
My family, on the other hand, hardly
ever seemed to be at home.
From as far back as I can remember,
my parents travelled the world with
their international reconciliation work,
leaving Diggie and me for weeks,
sometimes months,
at a time.
Now Diggie and I are the ones who are
gone.

In Iowa,
my world is falling apart.
My marriage is on the rocks.
Thank God for my job at the
university library and my master's
degree in English Literature
(I bury myself in that damn thesis).

And I take every stage role I can get
my hands on.

TAKE DRESS OFF MANNEQUIN

As writing was Emily's passion,
so acting is mine,
and has been ever since I saw my first
play when I was four years old
and announced to my parents the next
day that

**THROW DRESS OVER SHOULDER, FAN OUT
PLEATS; CHILD'S VOICE**

I was going to be an actress when I
grew up.

**TRANSFORM BACK TO ADULT; MOVE STOOL,
JUST *US* OF PILE OF PAPERS AND SIT**

We had a brilliant dress-up box at
home, and I would improvise
one-*girl* shows,
and make my parents watch,
performing all the other voices behind
my hand.

**BRING LEFT HAND UP TO HIDE MOUTH,
LOOKING *OSL*; TRANSFORM MOMENTARILY
INTO WICKED SISTER**

> Cinderella!
> Have you finished my dress yet?!

TRANSFORM BACK

> Ever since I first met Emily,
> I have wanted to be her.

> Well…
> portray her.

**START TO SLOWLY SLIDE DRESS OFF SHOULDER
ONTO LAP; THIS HAS A MYSTERIOUS EFFECT
ON EDIE**

> No…

**BECAUSE OF THE FEEL OF THE DRESS AND THE
MOVEMENT OF HER WORDS, EDIE EXPERIENCES
A SHIFT OF REALITY**

> Be
> Her.

**MORE IS HAPPENING, SHE TAKES HER TIME;
ETERNITY IS BREATHING**

    Get

    inside

    Emily's

    dress…

**SOMETHING…
SOMETHING…
EDIE GASPS**

    Perhaps I am her!
    Oh my God, that's it!
    I'm her latest incarnation!

    Ok, ok,
    what do I know about reincarnation?
    Um, you keep coming back, living as
    many lives as it takes, until you get
    everything right and reach
    Enlightenment.
    Oh,
    and Karma.
    Uh,

Negative Karma:
The things I didn't figure out in my
last life I have to try and figure out in
this one.
And Positive Karma:
The stuff I did get right in my last
life…
I don't have to bother with in this one.

Like cooking!

**THREAD NEEDLE AND BEGIN SEWING LACE
ONTO DRESS AND REMOVING PINS**

In my last life as Emily,
I loved to cook,
'my father would eat no bread but
mine'.
So, in this life…
I let my husband do it all.

Housecleaning.
In my last life as Emily,
I hated housework.
But,
one rung up the enlightenment ladder,
in this life I have quite grown to enjoy
it.

Maybe in my next incarnation I won't
have to do it at all.

Sewing.
Hmmmm…
Emily didn't say much about sewing.
She just did it.
Which is probably why I'm still just
doing it.

Gardening.
In my last life as Emily I had two
green thumbs.
I was in charge of the garden and the
conservatory at the Homestead and I
knew my plants inside out.
So…
in this life…
I…stick a few bulbs in the ground,
and I do love wandering through,
and appreciating,
other people's gardens.

CRINGE

Music.
In my last life as Emily I loved to play
the piano. My father bought me one

when I was 14.
I even improvised my own tunes.
Which would explain why I was so
resistant to taking piano lessons in this
life to the point of driving my mother
to tears.
I knew I didn't need to learn the piano
again in this incarnation.

Poetry.
In my last life as Emily I did a
prodigious amount of writing.
But in this life
my desire is to interpret the written
word on the stage.
Maybe that's why I'm trying to write a
play about Emily,
so that I can speak aloud the words I
wrote in silence in my last incarnation.
Ooo,

LITTLE SHIVER...

I like that.

Panic.
In my last life as Emily I struggled
with panic and didn't resolve it.
So,

Karma,
that's why I'm still struggling with
panic in this life and the way things
are going…
I'll be back for another round.

Oh!
Why didn't I think of this before??
Emily Dickinson.
E m i l y
D i c k i n s o n.
'E'-'D'?
That's my name.
Edie.
Get it?
Emily sometimes signed her letters
with just her initials.
'E.D.'

Oh—speaking of letter writing,
I was quite a prolific letter writer in
this life when I was younger,
not as prolific as in my last life as
Emily,
with 93 correspondents,
but I did have one particular pen
friend.
An American girl, actually.

She and I wrote to each other about
everything.
Just like Emily and Sue!
Funnily enough
I married my pen friend's brother and
moved to America.

STOP SEWING...

Hang on a minute...

I married my penfriend's brother and
moved to America.
Sue married Emily's brother and
moved next door.
Ohhh I'm not Emily!
I'm Sue!!

MORTIFIED; RETURN TO SEWING

Well it was a stupid idea anyway.

PAUSE

Not even sure I believe in
reincarnation.

PAUSE

But the panic attacks are real.

**STOP SEWING; PLACE DRESS ON PILE OF
PAPERS AND CROSS TO STACK OF BOOKS** *DSL*

> Emily didn't call them that, but this
> letter to Sue about going to church
> alone certainly sounds like one to me:

**KNEEL AND PICK UP BOOK OF EMILY'S
LETTERS; FIND LETTER; READ**

> *I'm just from meeting, Susie, and as I sorely
> feared, my 'life' was made a 'victim'. I reached
> the steps. How big and broad the aisle seemed,
> full huge enough before, as I quaked slowly
> up — and reached my usual seat!*
> *And there I sat, and sighed, and wondered I
> was scared so, for surely in the whole world
> was nothing I need to fear — Yet there the
> Phantom was, and though I kept resolving to be
> as brave as Turks, and bold as Polar Bears, it
> did'nt help me any. During the exercises I
> became more calm, and got out of church quite
> comfortably. Several roared around, and,
> sought to devour me, but I fell an easy prey to
> Miss D., being too much exhausted to make any
> farther resistance.*
> *She entertained me with much sprightly
> remark, until our gate was reached, and I*

need'nt tell you Susie, just how I clutched the
latch, and whirled the merry key, and fairly
danced for joy, to find myself at home*!*

**PUT BOOK DOWN, RETURN TO STOOL, SIT AND
RESUME SEWING**

At home.
Hmph.
My panic attacks
started
'at home'
every time my parents left on one of
their international reconciliation trips.
They acted as if they were going down
to the corner shop to buy a loaf of
bread.
'Everything will be all right.
You'll be fine.'

How do they know?
How can anyone promise that?
Don't you read the newspapers?
Watch the news?
Terrible things happen all the time.

Please don't go.

I tried to tell myself good things
happen all the time, too.
But it didn't help me.
Any.

Nothing helped.

**SLOWLY, A COLD BLUE LIGHT COMES UP *SL*;
SLOWLY TURN GAZE TO THE LIGHT LAYING
SEWING ON LAP; PAUSE; SLOWLY BRING LEFT
HAND UP TO COVER MOUTH**

> *Of Course—I prayed—*
> *And did God Care?*
> *He cared as much as on the Air*
> *A Bird—had stamped her foot—*
> *And cried 'Give Me'—*

BLUE LIGHT FADES; SLOWLY RESUME SEWING

Panic begins at the back of my neck,
shoots across the top of my skull and
plunges into the pit of my stomach.
Then the cold sweats start
and the dizziness
and the shortness of breath.
And then the shaking.
Huge uncontrollable spasms.
My jaw so tight I can barely speak.

I have to die or find another way to
live.
The cost is too high.
It takes me days to recover.
Public places,
especially when combined with
travelling,
like airports,
are the worst.

Perhaps Emily's solution was to
become a recluse.
At times it's an extremely attractive
option.

But Emily could pursue her passion,
writing,
at home.
I can't pursue my passion,
acting,
if I shut myself away.

But how do I get to the theatre when I
can't get on public transport or go out
after dark—because of course that's
when 'the most terrible things
happen'.
Afraid of what I might see and hear,

afraid of throwing up in reaction to it
and never being able to stop,
or worse still,
afraid of losing my mind and never
being able to come back.

> *The first Day's Night had come —*
> *And grateful that a thing*
> *So terrible — had been endured —*
> *I told my Soul to sing —*
>
> *She said her Strings were snapt —*
> *Her Bow — to Atoms blown —*
> *And so to mend her — gave me work*
> *Until another Morn —*

STOP SEWING

> *And then — a Day as huge*
> *As Yesterdays in pairs,*
> *Unrolled its horror in my face —*
> *Until it blocked my eyes —*
>
> *My Brain — begun to laugh —*
> *I mumbled — like a fool —*
> *And tho' 'tis Years ago — that Day —*
> *My Brain keeps giggling — still.*

And Something's odd—within—
That person that I was—
And this One—do not feel the same—

RESUME SEWING

Could it be Madness—this?

SILENCE

Perhaps that's why I act.
So I won't go mad.

Speaking of which, did you know that
per capita the artistic professions have
the highest rate of manic-depressives
and schizophrenics?

But I digress.

PAUSE

One route to enlightenment Emily
didn't choose was the religious one
at a time when it was expected,
when there were numerous Christian
revivals in Amherst,
when all her friends and family joined
the church.
Emily wrote:

We told you we did not learn to pray — but
then our freckled bosom bears it's friends — in
it's own way — to a simpler sky —

Emily's school was divided into
'Christians,
Hopers,
and
No-hopers'.

Emily was the only
No-hoper left at the end of year.
When all who had

MOMENTARY TENT REVIVAL EVANGELIST'S
VOICE

'Found their saviour in Christ'

were asked to rise,
Emily firmly remained seated,
much to the astonishment of the
assembly.
But Emily thought

a lie would be queerer.

When I was 14, I was also asked to
rise.

Unlike Emily,
I
stood
up.

But then
things…
shifted,
and I sat down again about ten years
later.

Emily stopped going to church
altogether.
Her religion was in Nature
and Beauty
and Life with a capital 'L':

> *I find ecstasy in living — the mere sense of living*
> *is joy enough.*
> *I often wonder how the love of Christ, is*
> *done — when that — below — holds — so —*

An avowed pagan,
Emily preferred her garden and the
fields to any church:

> *If God had been here this summer, and seen*
> *the things that I have seen — I guess that He*

*would think His Paradise superfluous. Don't
tell Him, though, for after all He's said about
it, I should like to see what He was building
for us.*

Emily remained true to herself and her
convictions,
no small accomplishment.
And the pain and the joy of that is so
evident in her poems.

PICK UP BOOK, FIND POEM AND READ

*I'm ceded — I've stopped being Theirs —
The name They dropped upon my face
With water, in the country church
Is finished using, now,
And They can put it with my Dolls,
My childhood, and the string of spools,
I've finished threading — too —*

*Baptized, before, without the choice,
But this time, consciously, of Grace —
Unto supremest name —
Called to my Full — The Crescent dropped —
Existence's whole Arc, filled up,
With one small Diadem.*

My second Rank — too small the first —
Crowned — Crowing — on my Father's breast —
A half unconscious Queen —
But this time — Adequate — Erect,
With Will to choose, or to reject,
And I choose, just a Crown —

PAUSE

1993.
The summer of the Great Midwestern
flood.
Iowa is virtually underwater.
And so am I.
After four and a half years of trying to
make my marriage work,
I have to leave my husband before I go
under.

The summer repertory theatre I am
acting with has to postpone its final
performances because the parking lot
has become part of the Iowa River and
there are catfish in the basement.

THROUGHOUT THE FOLLOWING, EDIE LOOKS
TERRIFIED *DSR* ON 'AIRPORTS', THEN *DSL* ON
'PANIC'; AS THESE PROGRESS, THEY BECOME

**LESS LOUD BUT MORE AND MORE PHYSICALLY
INTENSE, AS THOUGH EDIE IS TRYING TO
HOLD HERSELF TOGETHER; THE 'AIRPORT',
'PANIC' BECOME NO MORE THAN A SQUEAK,
EVEN SILENT BY THE END; EDIE RECOVERS
FROM EACH EPISODE WHILE SHE CONTINUES
SPEAKING**

> I go home to London.
> AIRPORTS!
> PANIC!

RECOVERING

> When I walk in the door, I am shocked
> by the physical and mental
> deterioration in my Dad,
> who is by now suffering quite severely
> from the Alzheimer-like Binswangers
> disease.
>
> One day Mum calls me into the
> kitchen.
> A shadow has been found on her
> mammogram.
> I have to go back to Iowa to finish the
> summer rep shows,
> but I tell her if she needs me,
> I'll come home.

Back in Iowa City…
AIRPORTS!
PANIC!

RECOVERING

…the floods have abated and I finish
the plays.
I get the call from Mum.
It's malignant.

I fly back to London…
AIRPORTS!
PANIC!

RECOVERING

…at the beginning of September,
expecting to stay only six weeks.
I stay all the way through Christmas
and nine days into the New Year.

To give Mum a break,
I take over responsibility for Dad's care.

Emily's mother was an invalid for
many years and Emily was her chief
nurse. After her mother's death Emily
wrote:

We were never intimate Mother and Children
while she was our Mother—but Mines in the
same Ground meet by tunneling and when she
became our Child, the Affection came—

Not that Dad and I hadn't been
affectionate father and daughter,
but there is a new love that comes
when he becomes the child.
And child he has become.
Overwhelmed by the 24-hour care he
now needs,
Mum and I take the difficult decision
to place him in a nursing home.
Mum goes in for her surgery the same
afternoon I take Dad to the home.
Dad had been a medical doctor,
but now can do nothing to support my
Mum.
In fact,
he is completely unaware that she is ill
at all.
But, Mum's operation is a success and
the prognosis is good.

1994.
I return to Iowa City...

AIRPORTS!
PANIC!

RECOVERING

…and move into an apartment of my
own.
Bliss!
I tell Mum I'll only stay in Iowa for
another six months,
take care of my divorce,
and then move back to London.
After all, what is there to keep me in
Iowa now?

Theatre!

I am cast in a play.
And then another.
And then another.
Every actor's dream—how can I walk
away from this?

In September,
my divorce is finally finalised,
and while in the play
Dancing at Lughnasa,
I surprise myself

completely
by falling in love with the actor,
called Jack,
who plays my senile older brother.
Also called Jack.

LOOK *SL*; LEFT HAND COVERS MOUTH

'Not another American!'
says Mum on the phone.
'Does this mean you're not coming
home?'

I do go home to London for
Christmas…
AIRPORTS!
PANIC!

RECOVERING

…and visit my Dad.
The last time I see him I am not sure
he knows who I am,
though he says he does when I ask.
When I leave,
he is watching TV,
seemingly oblivious to my departure.

Back in Iowa…
AIRPORTS!
PANIC!

RECOVERING

…I find myself telling Jack about Dad
more and more,
the stories just keep coming.
The Iowa winter makes me think of
Dad's love of the Canadian winters:
Huge snowfalls.
Bright sun.
Blizzards.
Temperatures well below freezing.
Starlit skies.
His boyhood on the Canadian prairies.
His taking Diggie and me sledding on
a six-foot wooden sled on a hill outside
Ottawa.

One night in February,
the 6th to be exact,
I get the call.

Dad
has died.

Jack and I go outside
and stand under the stars
in the snow
in the cold,
deep
blue
night.

STOP SEWING; LOOK OUT

> *We were eating our supper the fifteenth of June,*
> *and Austin came in. He had a despatch in his*
> *hand, and I saw by his face we were all lost,*
> *though I didn't know how. He said that father*
> *was very sick, and he and Vinnie must go. The*
> *train had already gone. While horses were*
> *dressing, news came he was dead.*
> *Father does not live with us now — he lives in a*
> *new house. Though it was built in an hour it is*
> *better than this. We take him the best flowers,*
> *and if we only knew he knew, perhaps we could*
> *stop crying.*
> *Though it is many nights, my mind never comes*
> *home.*

SILENCE

RESUME SEWING

One of my greatest fears as a child was
that Dad would die while he was away
on one of his trips, just as Emily's
father did. Now Dad had died
in his room
in the nursing home,
alone,
and I was the one who was away.

I fly home to London…

**LOOK *DSL*; NOTHING; PUZZLED, LOOK *DSR*;
STILL NOTHING; PUZZLED, BUT RELIEVED**

…No panic.

Diggie and I spend two weeks with
Mum.
The days following a death can be so
rich—
we laugh as much as we cry—
we tell each other our favourite stories
about Dad
and re-tell his terribly bad jokes.

FINISH SEWING

Emily chose not to attend her father's
funeral.

His Heart was pure and terrible and I think
no other like it exists. I am glad there is
Immortality — but would have tested it
myself — before entrusting him.

OPEN BOOK OF POEMS TO NO 1732 AND READ

My life closed twice before its close —
It yet remains to see
If Immortality unveil
A third event to me

So huge, so hopeless to conceive
As these that twice befell.
Parting is all we know of heaven,
And all we need of hell.

I miss Dad's laugh and his hands the
most.
Who will give me good books for
Christmas now?
I'm glad it wasn't Emily's father who
gave me books:

He buys me many Books — but begs me not to
read them — because he fears they joggle the
Mind.
He gave me quite a trimming about 'Uncle

Tom' and 'Charles Dickens' and and these 'modern Literati' who he says are nothing *compared to past generations, who flourished when* he was a boy. *So I'm quite in disgrace at present.*

RETURN BOOK TO FLOOR

During my time in London, I surprise myself yet again
by telling Mum and Diggie that I have decided to move in with Jack.

SET DRESS DOWN ON STOOL; TURN *US* TO EXIT, SPEAKING

Back in Iowa…

STOP, BECOMES RIGID. LOOK LEFT, THEN RIGHT

AIRPORTS!
PANIC!

DAMN!

EXIT

…we wash the windows and spring
clean Jack's little red cottage on the
banks of the Iowa River.

ENTER WITH IRONING BOARD AND GO TO *USL*

We paint the walls, rearrange the
furniture,

**IN ONE SWIFT MOVEMENT, OPEN IRONING
BOARD…**

and move my stuff in.

AND FIRMLY SET IT DOWN

EXIT

Jack loves to cook, so we strike a
bargain:

ENTER WITH IRON

He'll cook and I'll clean.

STOP

Karma.

PLUG IRON IN

I am happier than I've been in years,
yet in deep mourning for my Dad.

**PUT DRESS ON IRONING BOARD AND BEGIN TO
IRON PLEATS**

I turn to Emily once more and find
comfort in Emily's letters about her
father.
He had been a severe, Puritan New
Englander, and Emily wrote about the
things her father had done that had
surprised her:

STOP IRONING

*The last April that father lived, lived I mean
below, there were several snow-storms, and the
birds were so frightened and cold they sat by the
kitchen door. Father went to the barn in his
slippers and came back with a breakfast of
grain for each, and hid himself while he
scattered it, lest it embarrass them.*

Two years after her father's death she
wrote:

> *I dream about father every night, always a*
> *different dream, and forget what I am doing*
> *daytimes, wondering where he is. Without*
> *any body, I keep thinking. What kind can*
> *that be?*

RESUME IRONING

I find myself wrestling with my Dad's
legacy:
should I take up his international
reconciliation work where he left off?
Had I led him to believe I would?
Am I letting him down?
He sought above all to find and do
God's will;
is my vision,
my calling,
too small?

And then I have my own dream about
Dad.
We are sitting in a row of chairs
ranged along the wall in his nursing
home. He floats in and out of lucidity,
like a weak signal on the radio.

STOP IRONING; PLACE HANDS ON IRONING BOARD

> He asks me what I want to do with my
> life.
> 'Act,' I reply.

LOOK DOWN AT RIGHT HAND AND WATCH AS IT FLOATS TO COVER LEFT HAND

> He puts his hand on mine and says to
> me:
> 'Then do it with your whole heart.'

PAUSE; LOOK AT PILE OF PAPERS ON FLOOR
DSC

> Emily the play comes off the shelf.

RESUME IRONING WITH NEW ENTHUSIASM

> If I'm ever going to write it, I have to
> do so now or consign it to oblivion.
> Becky had sent me a complete copy of
> Emily's letters.
> It's the first time I have all of Emily's
> 1049 extant letters in one volume.
> I read them through

and am blown away.
Her letters are as well crafted as her
poems, and leave me breathless.
Just as her poems get shorter and more
concise over the years,
so do her letters,
as Emily distils everything down to its
essence.
I can't read them fast enough.
Here,

STOP IRONING; INDICATE BOOK OF LETTERS
DSL

in her letters—

GASP...NEW IDEA

—is Emily in her own words!

GO TO BOOK OF LETTERS AND PICK THEM UP

I can be her mouthpiece, after all!
I don't have to put words in her
mouth!

FLIP THROUGH PAGES

All I have to do is edit the 1049 extant
letters into a play!

SLAM BOOK CLOSED

What could be simpler?
I don't even have to do any writing;
it's already all here.

Except, of course, that I've never been
able to edit anything.
My essays at the Oxford Poly were
always far too long and as I could never
choose from all the quotes I'd amassed,
I just used them all.

So!
Where to begin?

Well, let's begin at the beginning.

TURN TO FIRST LETTER

Emily's first letter in the collection was
written to her brother Austin when she
was 11 years old.
Listen to this:

READ

> *The other day Francis brought your Rooster*
> *home and the other 2 went to fighting him*
> *while I was gone to School — mother happened*
> *to look out of the window and she saw him*
> *laying on the ground — he was most dead —*
> *but she and Aunt Elisabeth went right out*
> *and took him up and put him in a Coop and*
> *he is nearly well now — while he is shut up the*
> *other Roosters — will come around and insult*
> *him in Every possible way by Crowing right*
> *in his Ears — and then they will jump up on*
> *the Coop and Crow there as if they — wanted*
> *to show that he was Completely in their power*
> *and they could treat him as they chose — Aunt*
> *Elisabeth said she wished their throats would*
> *split and then they could insult him no*
> *longer —*

CLOSE VOLUME

Emily later described this Aunt
Elizabeth as

the only male relative on the female side.

So, that's the first letter and my
opening.

And I have an ending—

TURN TO FINAL LETTER

Emily's last letter, written to her
cousins, Fanny and Louise Norcross,
when she knew she was dying:

READ

> *Little Cousins,*
> *Called back.*
> *Emily.*

Talk about concise!

**CLOSE BOOK, SIT ON STOOL, PLACE BOOK ON
FLOOR**

Now all I have to do is fill in the
middle. It's just a matter of cutting
and pasting. So, I reread all 1049
letters and type into the computer the
ones I like the best, the ones that show
as many different facets of Emily as
possible.

PICK UP VERSION ONE FROM PILE OF PAPERS

That first version is—
nine
hours
long.
Not much longer than Nicholas
Nickleby,
but a little long for a one-person play.

TOSS VERSION ONE *DSL* ONTO FLOOR

But how to cut it down?
Many of Emily's letters don't stand on
their own without some sort of
explanation and how would the
audience keep track of who she was
writing to when?
I'd need extensive programme notes all
over again.
and slides…
and a flipchart…
and an overhead projector…

RETURNING TO IRONING

What if,
instead of trying to give an overview of
all the 93 people Emily wrote to,
I choose from her most frequent and
important correspondents?

STOP IRONING

Like Sue.
How did Emily's letters to Sue go from
this:

> *Oh Susie, my child, will you indeed come home*
> *next Saturday, and be my own again, and kiss*
> *me as you used to? I hope for you so much, and*
> *feel so eager for you, feel that I* cannot *wait,*
> *feel that* now *I must have you — that the*
> *expectation once more to see your face again,*
> *makes me feel hot and feverish, and my heart*
> *beats so fast — Why, Susie, it seems to me as if*
> *my absent Lover was coming home so soon —*
> *and my heart must be so busy, making ready*
> *for him.*

To this?

> *Sue — There is but one alternative — We differ*
> *often lately, and this must be the last.*
> *You need not fear to leave me lest I should be*
> *alone, for I often part with things I fancy I*
> *have loved, — sometimes to the grave, and*
> *sometimes to an oblivion bitterer than death.*
> *If it is finished, tell me, and I will raise the lid*
> *to my box of Phantoms, and lay one more love in.*

> *Few have been given me, and if I love them so,*
> *that for* idolatry, *they are removed from me — I*
> *simply murmur* gone, *and the billow dies*
> *away into the boundless blue, and no one knows*
> *but me, that one went down today.*

RESUME IRONING

Both those letters were written to Sue
before she married Austin and settled in
the Evergreens, next door to the
Homestead.
What Emily thought of the marriage
we don't know—
only a few oblique comments remain.
And there are no letters extant for the
first few years following the wedding,
which took place in New York State,
by the way,
and which none of Emily's family
attended—
well, except for Austin of course.

But notes flew back and forth between
the Homestead and the Evergreens for
the rest of Emily's life.
Many of Emily's letters have had their
references to Sue literally cut out of them,

possibly by Austin,
and only two of Sue's letters to Emily
remain,
both heavily censored.
Twenty years after their
correspondence began, Emily wrote
Sue one line:

'Egypt — thou knew'st' —

It's a quotation from Shakespeare, from
one of Anthony's speeches to
Cleopatra, and, for Becky and me, this
summed up Emily's relationship with
Sue:

STOP IRONING; LOOK OUT

'Egypt, thou
knew'st too well
My heart was to thy rudder tied by the
strings,
And thou shouldst tow me after: o'er
my spirit
Thy full supremacy thou knew'st, and
that
Thy beck might from the bidding of
the gods
Command me.'

97

RESUME IRONING

What really happened between those
two women
remains a mystery.

Oh! Speaking of mysteries, I haven't
told you about the Master letters.

STOP IRONING, SIT ON STOOL

There are three of them, and no one
knows who they were written to, or if
they were even sent, though there are
several candidates.

2ND GOSSIP — MRS SNOOT

'It was the Reverend Charles
Wadsworth, and rumour has it he
would not give up his wife or his
preaching for Emily.'

3RD GOSSIP — MR KNOWITALL

'No, no, no, it was Samuel Bowles,
charismatic newspaper editor and
married man, drawn to women with
spirit and brains.'

SHRUG

The three Master letters were written
over a period of three years, while
Emily was undergoing her emotional
crisis in her early thirties.
She feared going completely blind;
her poems were rejected for
publication;
her mother became an invalid;
several deaths deeply affected her;
and America was divided by the Civil
War.

The first Master letter is fairly stable.
The second
less so:

> *If you saw a bullet hit a Bird — and he told*
> *you he was'nt shot — you might weep at his*
> *courtesy, but you would certainly doubt his*
> *word.*
> *'Tell you of the want' — you know what a leech*
> *is, dont you — and Daisy's arm is small — and*
> *you have felt the horizon hav'nt you — and did*
> *the sea — never come so close as to make you*
> *dance?*

The third Master letter is the most
emotionally frayed.
But however close Emily came to a
complete breakdown,
her letters and poems remain
extremely well crafted.

> *Oh, did I offend it — Daisy — offend it — who*
> *bends her smaller life to his meeker every day —*
> *who only asks — a task — something to do for*
> *love of it — some little way she cannot guess to*
> *make that master glad —*
> *Daisy — who never flinched thro' that awful*
> *parting, but held her life so tight he should not*
> *see the wound — who would have sheltered him*
> *in her childish bosom — only it was'nt big eno'*
> *for a Guest so large — this Daisy — grieve her*
> *Lord —*
> *Low at the knee that bore her once unto wordless*
> *rest Daisy kneels a culprit — tell her her*
> *fault — Master — if it is small eno' to cancel*
> *with her life, she is satisfied — but punish dont*
> *banish her —*
> *Wonder wastes my pound, you said I had no*
> *size to spare —*
> *You send the water over the Dam in my brown*
> *eyes —*
> *I've got a cough as big as a thimble — but I*

dont care for that — I've got a Tomahawk in
my side but that dont hurt me much. Her
master stabs her more —

Well, whoever he was,

STAND

he was a jerk.

RETURN TO IRONING

Ok, so that's Sue,
and the Master letters.
But which other correspondents to
choose?
Well, Austin, of course.
Oh, and Thomas Wentworth
Higginson,
the man Emily hoped would publish
her poems.

Austin always said Emily posed in her
letters to Higginson.
My sister Diggie accuses me of the
same when I'm on the phone.

**PICK UP IRON AND USE IT AS A TELEPHONE,
SPEAKING WITH BREATHY, FALSE CONCERN**

'Hello?
Oh how WONderful.
No! Really?
Oh, that is maaaarvellous!'

PUT IRON DOWN

…No wonder she moved to Sweden!

**REMOVE DRESS FROM IRONING BOARD; HOLD
UP DRESS AGAINST SELF; STEP UP ONTO STOOL
CHECKING DRESS LENGTH ETC.**

Emily's coy, disingenuous, artfully
naïve responses to Higginson's direct
questions about herself and her family
are quite something:

**LOOK STRAIGHT OUT HOLDING DRESS UP AT
SHOULDERS**

> *I had no portrait, now, but am small, like the
> Wren, and my Hair is bold, like the Chestnut
> Bur—and my eyes, like the Sherry in the
> Glass, that the Guest leaves—Would this do
> just as well?*
> *You asked how old I was? I made no verse—
> but one or two—until this winter—Sir—*

DROP TOP OF DRESS TO WAIST

Liar!
She'd written over five hundred poems
by now.

RESUME PREVIOUS POSE

You inquire my Books—For Poets—I have
Keats—and Mr and Mrs Browning. For
Prose—Mr Ruskin—Sir Thomas Browne—
and the Revelations. I went to school—but in
your manner of the phrase—had no education.
You ask of my Companions Hills—Sir—and
the Sundown—and a Dog—large as myself,
that my Father bought me—They are better
than Beings—because they know—but do not
tell—and the noise in the Pool, at Noon, excels
my Piano. I have a Brother and Sister—My
Mother does not care for thought—and Father,
too busy with his Briefs—to notice what we
do—They are religious—except me—and
address an Eclipse, every morning—whom they
call their 'Father.'
I could not weigh myself—Myself—
My size felt small—to me—
Is this—Sir—what you asked me to tell you?

STEP OFF STOOL AND DRAPE DRESS OVER FRONT OF MANNEQUIN

Tell all the Truth but tell it slant —

said Emily.
She certainly seems to be the master of
that.

SIT ON STOOL

Emily had first written to Higginson
in response to an article he had written
in the *Atlantic Monthly* entitled
'Letter to a Young Contributor',
giving advice on how to get published.
She enclosed four poems and a note:

*Are you too deeply occupied to say if my Verse is
alive?
The Mind is so near itself — it cannot see,
distinctly — and I have none to ask —
Should you think it breathed — and had you
the leisure to tell me, I should feel quick
gratitude —
If I make the mistake — that you dared to tell
me — would give me sincerer honor — toward
you —*

I enclose my name—asking you, if you please—
Sir—to tell me what is true?

Turned out Higginson had no ear for
her poetry,
couldn't see the genius in it.
He referred to her as 'my half crack'd
poetess'.
He was somewhat persuaded when
Mabel, Austin's mistress,
read him some of Emily's poetry after
Emily's death.
He reluctantly agreed to co-edit the
first volume of Emily's poetry that
Mabel published,
and was stunned by its success.

Right. So, I've got Sue and the Master
letters, Austin and Higginson so far.

**PICK UP SOME OF THE PAPERS AND START
RIFLING THROUGH THEM**

Oh! But the problem with choosing
just a few correspondents for the play
is what to do with the letters I can't
bear to part with.

STAND

Letters like this one:

Dear Dr. and Mrs Holland.

He was an editor of the newspaper *The Springfield Republican...*

> *I love to write to you — it gives my heart a holiday and sets the bells to ringing. I thought of you all last week, until the world grew rounder than it sometimes is, and I broke several dishes.*
> *Monday, I solemnly resolved I would be* sensible, *so I wore thick shoes. One glimpse of* The Republican *makes me break things again — I read in it every night.* [It] *seems to us like a letter from you, and we break the seal and read it eagerly.*
> *Who writes those funny accidents, where railroads meet each other unexpectedly, and gentlemen in factories get their heads cut off quite informally? The author, too, relates them in such a sprightly way, that they are quite attractive. Vinnie was disappointed to-night, that there were not more accidents —*

Or this, written to her cousins, the
Norcross sisters, during the American
Civil War:

> *Brave Frazer—'killed at Newbern,' darlings.*
> *His big heart shot away by a 'minie ball'. I*
> *had read of those—I didn't think Frazer*
> *would carry one to Eden with him. Just as he*
> *fell, in his soldier's cap, with his sword at his*
> *side, Frazer rode through Amherst. Classmates*
> *to the right of him, and classmates to the left of*
> *him, to guard his narrow face! He fell by the*
> *side of Professor Clark, his superior officer—*
> *lived ten minutes in a soldier's arms, asked*
> *twice for water—murmured just, 'My God!'*
> *and passed! Sanderson, his classmate, made a*
> *box of boards in the night, put the brave boy in,*
> *covered with a blanket, rowed six miles to reach*
> *the boat, —so poor Frazer came. They tell that*
> *Colonel Clark cried like a child, and could*
> *hardly resume his post.*
> *The bed on which he came was enclosed in a*
> *large casket shut entirely, and covered from*
> *head to foot with the sweetest flowers. He went*
> *to sleep from the village church. Crowds came to*
> *tell him goodnight, choirs sang to him, pastors*
> *told how brave he was—early-soldier heart.*
> *And the family bowed their heads, as the reeds*

the wind shakes.
Austin is stunned completely. Let us love better,
children, it's most that's left to do.

And I can't leave this one out:
A reply to a Valentine Emily wrote to a
cousin of hers when she was 18, and
which he had printed in the local
student newspaper:

Cousin William,
A little condescending, & sarcastic, your
Valentine to me, I thought; a little like an
Eagle, stooping to salute a Wren, & I concluded
once, I dared not answer it, for it seemed to me
not quite becoming — in a bird so lowly as
myself — to claim admittance to an Eyrie, &
conversation with it's King.
But I have changed my mind —
Sir, I desire an interview; meet me at sunrise, or
sunset, or the new moon — In gold, or in purple,
or sackcloth — With sword, or with pen, or
with plough — With soul, or spirit, or body.
With host or alone, in sunshine or storm, in
heaven or earth, — some how or no how — I
propose, sir, to see you.
And not to see *merely, but a chat, sir, or a tete-*
a-tete, a confab, a mingling of opposite minds is

what I propose to have. I feel sir that we shall
agree. We will be David and Jonathan, or
Damon and Phythias or what is better than
either, the United States of America.
That's what they call a metaphor in our
country. Don't be afraid of it, sir, it won't bite.

RETURN TO IRONING BOARD

I can't part with letters like these.

SPREAD PAPERS OVER IRONING BOARD

What if I pretend these letters were
written to one of the correspondents
I've already chosen?

Or is that cheating?

Is that too much poetic licence?

Does the end justify the means?

Yes!

LOOK AT DRESS ON MANNEQUIN

Tell all the Truth but tell it slant—

RETURN TO STOOL, SIT

I'm still not putting words in her
mouth after all,
I'm just rearranging them a little.

So,

PICK UP REMAINING VERSIONS OF THE PLAY

with a bit of poetic licence,
I keep editing.
I get my nine-hour version down to six
hours.

THROW VERSION TWO ONTO FLOOR

Then, three and-a-half.

THROW VERSION THREE ONTO FLOOR

And then,
finally,
after much ruthless cutting,
down to two.

THROW VERSION FOUR ONTO FLOOR

I find a director who agrees to work on
the play with me.
We give readings for theatre friends—
actors, playwrights—
but keep getting the same feedback:
'Incredible material but you haven't
got a play.
It doesn't go anywhere.
There's no plot.
Emily's language is so rich,
like really good chocolate,
you can only take in so much at a time.
But don't give up.
It's a good idea.'

DURING THE FOLLOWING, EDIE TAKES STOOL
BEHIND SCREEN (THROUGH WHICH SHE IS
VISIBLE) AND UNDRESSES

I
am
stuck.
Can't see the wood for the trees.
How to convey the length and breadth
and depth of Emily?
How to distil Emily down to her
essence?

Emily wrote:

> *While my thought is undressed — I can make*
> *the distinction, but when I put them in the*
> *Gown — they look alike, and numb.*
> *And when I try to organize — my little Force*
> *explodes — and leaves me bare and charred —*

I part ways,
amicably,
with the director.
She can't find her way into the script.

I ask Jack to take over.

LEAN OUT FROM SCREEN

Remember Jack?
The actor who cooks?

RETURN BEHIND SCREEN

But he can't find his way into the play
either.

By insisting on using only Emily's words,
I have created a problem for myself I
don't know how to solve.

I am so stuck, that
Emily gets put on the shelf yet again.
Maybe,
while I'm not looking,
a script will be born.

Or maybe
there is
no
play.

REACH FROM BEHIND SCREEN AND REMOVE DRESS FROM MANNEQUIN

I keep talking about wanting to
portray Emily.
To become her.
To be her.

PUT ON DRESS

But even when I put on Emily's dress,
it's still me inside the dress.
The actor's eternal dilemma.

1996.
Jack and I marry on the banks of the
Iowa River.

1997.
We move to England.
Back here, where the whole Emily play
idea started,
I have to have another go.
Another reading.
This time for Becky,
my original collaborator,
and two more theatre friends.
Same feedback
with some new advice:
'Put it on Radio 4 in instalments.
The letters are great radio material,
but you haven't got a play.'

Two other friends give a Christmas tea
and invite me to perform Emily.
I chop it down from two hours to 45
minutes.

**THROW 45-MINUTE VERSION OF PLAY OVER
SCREEN ONTO FLOOR**

Agony!
But get the same feedback.
Same radio advice, even.

LEAN OUT FROM SCREEN

Not a bad idea actually.
I should follow up on that.
Send a proposal in to Radio 4.

RETURN BEHIND SCREEN, RESUME CHANGING

But I need to get the stage play out of
my system first,
somehow.
I'm still not convinced it can't be done.

1998.
Jack and I move house and Emily
languishes in a box
and then a chest
for nine months.

1999.
Over supper one night,
I finally decide to talk to Jack about
the play again.
He asks,

WITH AMERICAN ACCENT

'Are you talking to me as a director?
If so, make an appointment with me,
bring all your Emily material,

and we'll discuss it.
Now, finish your supper.'

Sunday morning.
Eleven o'clock.
I gather all my versions of Emily in my
arms,
walk into the centre of the living
room,
and throw them down on the floor in
frustration.

'There she is,'
I say.

'And that,'
says Jack,
'is your opening line!'

CHECK SELF IN UPSTAGE MIRROR; TAKE IN
REFLECTION FULLY

There she is.

ENTER FROM BEHIND SCREEN; SURVEY SCENE;
MOVE TO CHEST, PICK UP SEVERAL 'SEWN
PAGES'; CHOOSE ONE; GLANCE THROUGH
PAGES, SEARCHING FOR A PARTICULAR POEM;

FIND IT; STAND AND MOVE *CS*; KNEEL ON TOP
OF PAPERS

PAUSE; BEGIN READING

> *I reckon — when I count at all —*
> *First — Poets — Then the Sun —*
> *Then Summer — Then the Heaven of God —*
> *And then — the List is done —*

LOOK OUT

> *But, looking back — the First so seems*
> *To Comprehend the Whole —*
> *The Others look a needless Show —*
> *So I write — Poets — All —*

TURN TO SEWING BOX, FIND NEEDLE AND
THREAD; START TO SEW PAGES TOGETHER IN A
BOOKLET; LIGHTS FADE TO...

BLACKOUT

Source acknowledgements

Dickinson poems are reprinted by permission of the publishers and the Trustees of Amherst College from the following volumes: *The Poems of Emily Dickinson*, Thomas H. Johnson, ed., Cambridge, MA: The Belknap Press of Harvard University Press, copyright © 1951, 1955, 1979, 1983 by the President and Fellows of Harvard College.

Dickinson letters are reprinted by permission of the publisher from *The Letters of Emily Dickinson*, edited by Thomas H. Johnson, Cambridge, MA: The Belknap Press of Harvard University Press, copyright © 1958, 1986 by the President and Fellows of Harvard College.

Sources of quotations

I don't know of anything so mighty (page 27)
   *The Lyman Letters: New Light on Emily Dickinson
   and her Family*, Richard B. Sewall, Amherst, MA,
   University of Massachussetts Press, 1965
It dropped so low in — my Regard— (page 33)
   Poem 747
I Measure every Grief I meet (page 35)
   Poem 561
I do not ask (page 38)
   Letter 246
The first section of Darkness (page 38)
   Letter 874
I must tell you about the character of Amherst (page 44)
   Mabel Loomis Todd letter to Mr and Mrs Loomis,
   6 November 1881, Mabel Loomis Todd Papers,
   Manuscripts and Archives Department, Yale
   University Library, Connecticut. Reprinted with
   permission.
All men say 'What' to me (page 50)
   Letter 271
shunned Men and Women (page 50)
   Letter 271
if you talk with no one (page 51)
   Letter 54